My Holiday in

India

Jane Bingham

WAYLAND

Published in paperback in 2014 by Wayland
Copyright © Wayland 2014

Wayland
338 Euston Road
London NW1 3BH

Wayland Australia
Level 17/207 Kent Street
Sydney NSW 2000

Produced for Wayland by
White Thomson Publishing Ltd
www.wtpub.co.uk
+44 (0)843 2087 460

Senior Editor: Victoria Brooker
Editors: Jane Bingham/Steve White-Thomson
Designer: Ian Winton
Map artwork: Stefan Chabluk
Proofreader: Alice Harman

British Library Cataloguing in Publication Data
Bingham, Jane
   My holiday in India.
   1. Vacations--India--Juvenile literature.
   2. India--Juvenile literature.
   I. Title II. India
   915.4'04532

   ISBN 978 07502 8314 4

Wayland is a division of Hachette Children's Books,
an Hachette UK company.

Printed in Malaysia

10 9 8 7 6 5 4 3 2 1

Cover: Taj Mahal: Shutterstock/Sahani Photography;
Dancer: Shutterstock/JeremyRichards.

p.1: Shutterstock/Regien Paassen; p.5: Dreamstime/
Pietrach; p.6: Shutterstock/saiko3p; p.7: Shutterstock/
JinYoung Lee; p.8: Dreamstime/Rene Drouyer; p.9:
Shutterstock/VLADJ55; p.10: Dreamstime/Subhra2jyoti;
p.11 (top): Shutterstock/joeborg; p.11 (bottom):
Shutterstock/Hung Chung Chih; p.12: Shutterstock/
paul prescott; p.13 (top): Dreamstime/Yue Liu; p.13
(bottom): Dreamstime/Mathes; p.14 (top): Dreamstime/
Stunnedmullett; p.14 (middle): Dreamstime/Rechitan
Sorin; p.14 (bottom): Dreamstime/Xin Hua; p.15 (top):
Dreamstime/Ajay Bhaskar; p.15 (bottom): Dreamstime/
Ajay Bhaskar; p.16: Shutterstock/Sahani Photography;
p.17: Shutterstock/Tereshchenko Dmitry; p.18 (top):
Shutterstock/NCG; p.18 (bottom): Dreamstime/Prashant
Vaidya; p.19 (top): Dreamstime/David Evison; p.19
(bottom): Shutterstock/NCG; p.20: Shutterstock/Regien
Paassen; p.21: Shutterstock/neelsky; p.22: Dreamstime/
Pixattitude; p.23: Shutterstock/JeremyRichards; p.24:
Dreamstime/John Kasawa; p.25: Dreamstime/Mangalika;
p.26 (top): Dreamstime/Beat Germann; p.26 (bottom):
Dreamstime/Indianeye; p.27 (top): Dreamstime/Rechitan
Sorin; p.27 (middle): Dreamstime/Jorisvo; p.27 (bottom):
Dreamstime/Nilanjan Bhattacharya; p.28: Dreamstime/
Aleksandar Todorovic; p.29 (top): Dreamstime/Samrat35;
p.29 (middle): Dreamstime/Danielal; p.29 (bottom):
Dreamstime/Beetle2k42; p.30: Dreamstime/Indiatraveler.

Contents

This is India!

India is a large country in the **continent** of Asia. Most visitors arrive there by aeroplane.

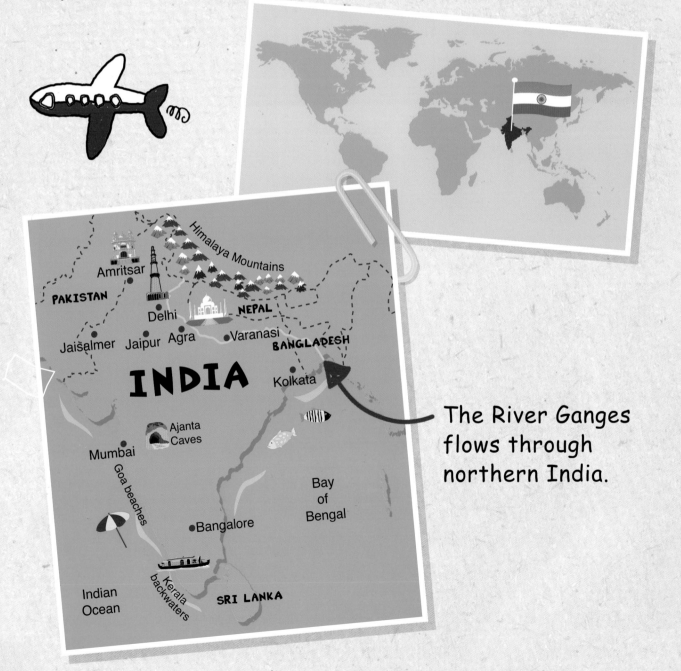

The River Ganges flows through northern India.

This busy street is in Mumbai.

Arriving in India is very exciting. The streets are full of people!

People in India speak many languages, but the main language is Hindi.

Speak Hindi!

hello/greetings
namaste (nah-mas-**teh**)

goodbye
namaskar (nah-mas-**kar**)

good/okay!
accha (ah-**chah**)

5

Sun and rain

In many parts of India, the climate is **tropical**, with hot, steamy weather.

Monsoon warning!

In the **monsoon season**, from June to September, there are heavy showers almost every day.

The tropical climate of Southern India is perfect for growing tea.

In northern India, it gets quite cold in December and January. But it starts to warm up again in February.

In the far north, it is very cold in winter. The Himalaya Mountains are covered with snow.

We visited Ladakh in the far north of India. It was sunny in the daytime but really cold at night!

7

Somewhere to stay

This hotel on a lake used to be a palace.

Most visitors to India stay in hotels. Some Indian hotels are very beautiful.

Indian kingdoms

In the past, India was divided into many kingdoms. Kings, called maharajas, lived in beautiful palaces.

In Kerala, on the south-west coast, you can spend the night on a boat!

This houseboat has a roof made from **rushes**. It travels through narrow rivers, called backwaters.

It was fun sleeping on a houseboat. I felt as if I was being rocked to sleep!

Travelling around

The quickest way to travel around India is by plane. But it's fun to take some train trips too.

Travelling by train gives you the chance to enjoy the countryside.

We went on a great train journey. I took lots of photos out of the window.

In the cities, you can ride in an auto rickshaw.

Auto rickshaws are often known as tuk-tuks, because their engines make a tuk-tuk sound.

Or you can jump on the back of a cycle rickshaw.

Cycle rickshaws are a great way to travel – if you're not in a great hurry!

City sights

Delhi is the capital city of India. It has some beautiful palaces, **mosques** and **forts**.

The Red Fort was built in the 1600s by a ruler called Shah Jahan. He also built the Taj Mahal.

City treats

Enjoy the noise and fun of a busy street market.

Explore the Jantar Mantar, an open-air **observatory** in Delhi.

Walk on Chowpatty Beach in Mumbai at sunset.

The city of Mumbai has many British-style buildings. They were built when India was part of the **British Empire**.

The Victoria Terminus railway station was named after Queen Victoria.

Like all Indian cities, Mumbai has some enormous slums. These are areas where very poor people live.

Thousands of people live in this slum by the railway line.

Old and new

Indian cities have a fantastic mixture of old and new buildings.

The Qutb Minar in Delhi is nearly a thousand years old. It is the tallest prayer tower in India.

The fort at Jaisalmer, in northern India, dates from the 12th century. Many battles were fought there.

The Hawa Mahal in Jaipur, northern India, was built in 1799. Its name means 'Palace of the Winds'.

The city of Bangalore, in southern India, is the centre of India's computer industry. It has some exciting modern buildings.

Bangalore looks especially good at night.

New buildings are always appearing in Indian cities!

These skyscrapers are in Mumbai.

Tombs and caves

India's most famous building is the Taj Mahal. It was built in Agra, northern India, by the ruler Shah Jahan. He was so sad when his wife died that he built a beautiful palace to be her **tomb**.

The Taj Mahal is made from marble, a precious white stone.

We got up really early to see the Taj Mahal. When the sun rose, its walls looked pink!

The Ajanta Caves are cut into the face of a rocky cliff. In the past, they were used as temples by **Buddhist** monks.

The caves are decorated with amazing carvings.

Many religions

India is a country of many religions. **Hindus**, **Muslims**, **Sikhs**, Buddhists and Christians all have their own special buildings.

Temples and mosques

You will see many Hindu temples in India. The temples are covered with carvings of gods and goddesses.

The carvings on Hindu temples are often brightly painted.

Ganesha is a popular Hindu god. He has a human body and an elephant's head.

Sikh temples are called gurdwaras.

Muslims pray in mosques.

The Golden Temple at Amritsar, in northern India, is a very holy place for Sikhs.

India's largest mosque is the Jama Masjid mosque in Delhi.

Be prepared!

Before you enter a temple or mosque you must take off your shoes. You also need to cover your shoulders and legs.

A very special river

The River Ganges flows through northern India. Hindus believe it is a holy river. There are many temples on the river banks.

The city of Varanasi was built beside the River Ganges. It is full of Hindu temples.

We went on a boat ride at Varanasi. I saw lots of people bathing in the river.

Before the River Ganges reaches the sea, it divides into thousands of streams. This area is called the Sundarbans. It is a national park, where animals are kept safe from harm.

Tigers, leopards and crocodiles live in the Sundarbans National Park.

Wildlife spotting

See where The Jungle Book began – at the Kanha National Park

Spot a rhinoceros – at the Kaziranga National Park

Look out for elephants – at the Corbett National Park

21

Festival time!

Indians hold festivals all through the year. People wear colourful costumes and play music in the streets.

Even elephants dress up for festivals!

Most festivals have dancing, and there is special food to eat.

This dancer is performing at a spring festival.

Famous festivals

Makar Sankranti January A winter festival. Children fly paper kites.	Holi March A spring festival. People throw coloured water and powder at each other.	Diwali October A festival of lights. People light lamps and set off fireworks.	

Feeling hungry

Some Indian dishes are hot and spicy, but it doesn't matter if you don't like spicy food. There are lots of other delicious foods to choose from.

A typical Indian meal is rice and curry with some pieces of flatbread. Curries can be mild or spicy.

Flatbreads

Flatbreads are round and flat, like a pancake. Chapatis (chu-pat-ees), naans (narns) and parathas (par-ah-tahs) are all different types of flatbreads.

If you like sweet things, you will love Indian desserts. They are usually soft, sticky and sweet!

Indians make special sweets for festivals. These sweets are for the Hindu festival of Diwali.

On the menu

dahl (darl)
lentils in sauce

paneer (pan-eer)
soft, white cheese

lassi (lass-ee)
a drink made with yogurt and spices

Let's go shopping!

India has all sorts of shops, but if you want a handmade gift the smaller stalls are best.

The owner of this stall is selling objects made from shells.

You will need to pay in rupees. Rupee notes have a picture of Gandhi, a famous Indian leader.

There is a huge
choice of gifts
for sale.

You could buy a pair
of leather slippers,

a painted elephant,

or a handmade
puppet.

The choice is
up to you!

Time to relax

It feels good to relax after lots of travelling.

The beaches of Goa, on the west coast, are very popular with holiday-makers.

Don't forget to pack
- hat
- sun cream
- bottled water

If you have some spare time, there are lots of fun things to do in India.

You can buy some paper kites and have a kite race.

You can get your hands painted with Indian patterns.

Or you can find a cricket match to watch. You might even be asked to join in!

Make it yourself

People in Rajasthan, in north-west India, make colourful puppets and hold puppet shows. Why not make your own simple puppet and put on a show with your friends?

Rajasthani puppets have painted wooden faces and bodies made from cloth.

You will need:

- cardboard tube from a toilet roll
- colourful material
- felt-tip pens
- glue
- elastic band
- large needle
- strong thread

Step 1.
Draw a face on the tube. It can look friendly or scary!

Elastic band

Step 2.
Wrap some material around the bottom of the tube to make a long tunic. Use the elastic band to fix it in place.

Step 3.
Wrap material around the top of the tube to make a headscarf. Then glue it to the tube.

Step 4.
Use your needle to attach two long threads to the top of the tube. Knot the threads together to make your puppet strings.

Now you are ready for your puppet show!

Useful words

British Empire A large group of countries that were ruled by Britain in the past.

Buddhist Someone who follows the religion of Buddhism, and studies the teachings of Buddha.

continent One of seven large areas of land on the Earth. The seven continents are Africa, Antarctica, Asia, Australia, Europe, North America and South America.

fort A very strong building like a castle.

Hindu Someone who follows the religion of Hinduism, and prays to many gods.

monsoon season A time of year when there are very heavy rain showers.

mosque A building where Muslims worship and pray.

Muslim Someone who belongs to the religion of Islam, and studies the teachings of Muhammad.

observatory A place where people can study stars and planets.

rushes Tall grasses that grow on river banks.

Sikh Someone who follows the religion of Sikhism, which began in India.

tomb A place where someone is buried when they die.

tropical Hot and rainy.